Johnny Art

The Art of Johnny Swager

Johnny

A Production of
Enfantino Publishing
a division of Enfantino Inc.

Published to the book trade by
WHITE STAG PRESS

Copyrights

ISBN: 978-097925836-7

Library of Congress Control: 2008927055

Contributing writers
Jack Manick, Nancy Enfantino

Production and design
Richard Enfantino

Johnny Art: The Art of Johnny Swager
is owned and produced by
Enfantino Publishing
a division of Enfantino Inc.
Cupertino, California
www.enfantinopublishing.com
800 631-7506

Published to the book trade by
WHITE STAG PRESS
a division of
Publishers Design Group, Inc.
Roseville, California
www.publishersdesign.com
800.587.6666

Printed in China

Acknowledgements

I would like to thank Gary and Lillian Phillips, co-publishers of Johnny's art book, for introducing me to Johnny Swager. They saw the talent in this young artist, and knew that I would appreciate it.

I would also like to thank Johnny's parents, Steve and Coy for all of their hard work, and input into Johnny's art book.

When I first saw Johnny's artwork, I saw talent, and pure innocence. When I met Johnny, I saw the same two qualities, plus a very well adjusted, happy young boy, that just wants to paint. I am excited to be a part of this young artist's journey into the future..

—Richard Enfantino
Enfantino Publishing

Contents

The Gallery

5

Who is Johnny?

Stop the car! Stop the car! His high-pitched voice quivered with excitement as his mother pulled off the road and came to a full stop. The young boy's eyes darted back and forth across the paper covered wooden billboard, reading each word, digesting each sentence, and smiling at each picture. Moments later, his curiosity satisfied, the young boy refocused his gaze back to the front of the car where his mother sat patiently behind the steering wheel. OK Mommy, we can go.

As the car slowly eased back onto the road, the young boy's mother tried holding back a broad smile that was quickly forming across her face. To another Mom, pulling the car off the road to allow her son to read a billboard might have proven an annoyance, but not to this mother. She always encouraged her son's curiosity, enthusiasm and his boundless appetite to learn.

The young boy's curiosity, however, was exceeded only by his ability to express himself artistically with colored pencils, paint and paintbrushes.

By luck, or by the hand of a higher power, Johnny's art came to be known by fellow artist, and book publisher Richard Enfantino. His first comment upon seeing the rich colors and childlike innocence of the paintings and drawings was "Wow!" "It's art from the heart and soul of a child who is gifted beyond his years."

Who is this young gifted prodigy who sees life through the rose-colored glasses of a child, and is starting his journey through life, and captures those images on paper and canvas? He is destined to have a major impact in the art world of the 21st century. He is only seven years old! Who is this young artist?

Who is Johnny Swager?

The Story

Johnny was born on Sept 4, 2000 to Coy Swager and Duane Stephens. He grew up in Las Vegas, surrounded by a large family of aunts, uncles, cousins and grandparents, and now lives in Liberty Lake, Washington. In his pre-kindergarten days, Johnny spent much of his daytime hours with his maternal grandparents, while Coy worked.

Art was Johnny's passion...it was his special way of expressing himself. It was something that he liked to do, and he did it well. When asked if he wanted a gift for a special occasion, he would always ask for pencils, pastels, watercolors or acrylics. "Johnny probably has every colored pencil ever made," his mother would say.

When visiting his grandparents during the summer months, Johnny would ask "Grammy" for plain white drawing paper. It had to be the right make, and had to have the proper feel. Because he was so particular in his selection of paper to draw and paint on, his grandmother took him to the art store, and let him select his own.

Paint by number sets never interested Johnny because they confined him, and limited his creativity with paint and colors. Johnny preferred instead, to use his Imagination, a plain sheet of white paper, and either a pencil, pastel or paintbrush. He painted what he knew, what he saw, and what he felt. When painting in his art class, he accepted guidance from his art teacher, Miss Annette, but in the end, Johnny's work was always his own.

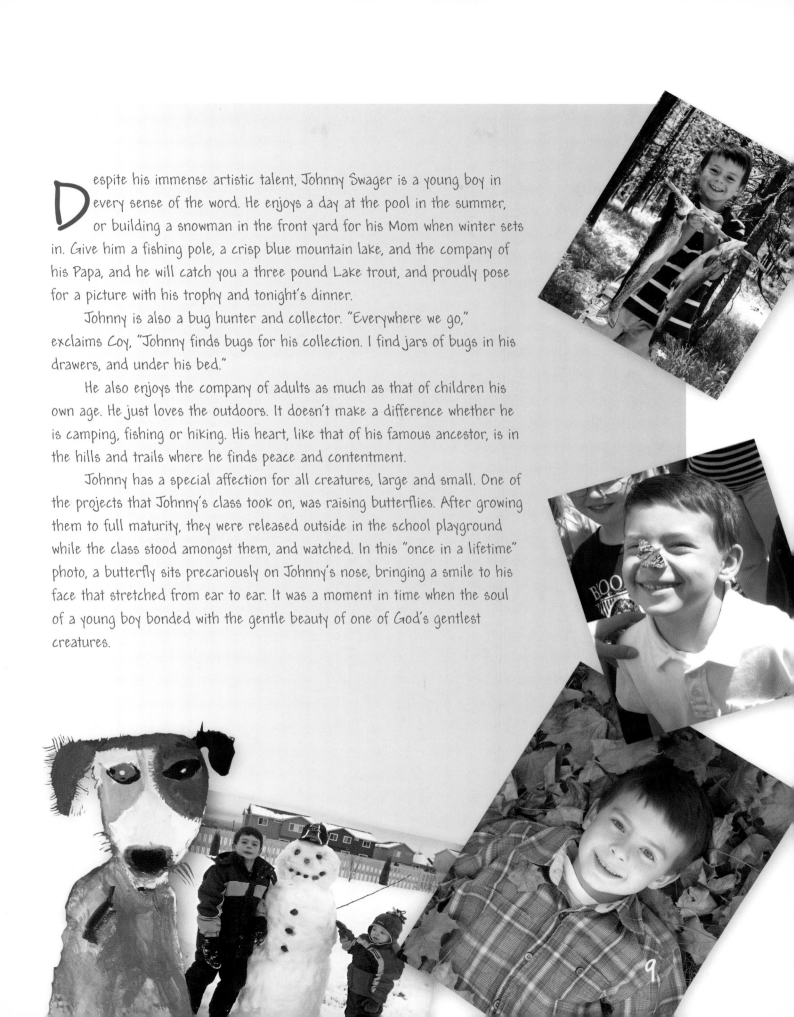

Despite his immense artistic talent, Johnny Swager is a young boy in every sense of the word. He enjoys a day at the pool in the summer, or building a snowman in the front yard for his Mom when winter sets in. Give him a fishing pole, a crisp blue mountain lake, and the company of his Papa, and he will catch you a three pound Lake trout, and proudly pose for a picture with his trophy and tonight's dinner.

Johnny is also a bug hunter and collector. "Everywhere we go," exclaims Coy, "Johnny finds bugs for his collection. I find jars of bugs in his drawers, and under his bed."

He also enjoys the company of adults as much as that of children his own age. He just loves the outdoors. It doesn't make a difference whether he is camping, fishing or hiking. His heart, like that of his famous ancestor, is in the hills and trails where he finds peace and contentment.

Johnny has a special affection for all creatures, large and small. One of the projects that Johnny's class took on, was raising butterflies. After growing them to full maturity, they were released outside in the school playground while the class stood amongst them, and watched. In this "once in a lifetime" photo, a butterfly sits precariously on Johnny's nose, bringing a smile to his face that stretched from ear to ear. It was a moment in time when the soul of a young boy bonded with the gentle beauty of one of God's gentlest creatures.

The Art

Some say that Johnny's artistic talents are God given. That must certainly be true, for Johnny is a direct descendant of Charles Marion Russell also known as C. M. Russell. He was one of the great artists of the American West. Russell created more than 2,000 paintings of cowboys, Indians, and landscapes set in the Western United States, in addition to bronze sculptures. Coy's Grandmother, Shirley E. Russell DeWiner is directly related to Charles M. Russell, and is an accomplished painter in her own right.

At age 3, he made a scrapbook, along with Mom's help. "Anything to do with paper, glue, scissors, and pencils, would occupy Johnny for hours. Johnny spent the day with Grammy and surprised his Mother with a vase of flowers he picked in Grammy's yard, and a picture he drew of them.

By age 4, Johnny was begging his mother to let him go to school. This is an experience that most kids dread...but not Johnny. During his pre-kindergarten classes, Johnny's teacher drew figures on the board, and asked her students to try to draw their versions of it. Johnny's drawings astounded not only his teacher but also his Mom.

"The Art Chalet", in downtown Liberty Lake, is where Johnny is currently taking his art lessons. His teacher, Annette Carter, says of Johnny, "Johnny has exhibited a talent for art such as I have never seen before in a seven year old. He is talented and gifted. Art just seems to come naturally to him. He needs nothing more than a plain white piece of paper and something to draw or paint with. His imagination and his God given talent do the rest."

ugs
are
Cool!

I ♥ Bugs

Johnny

12

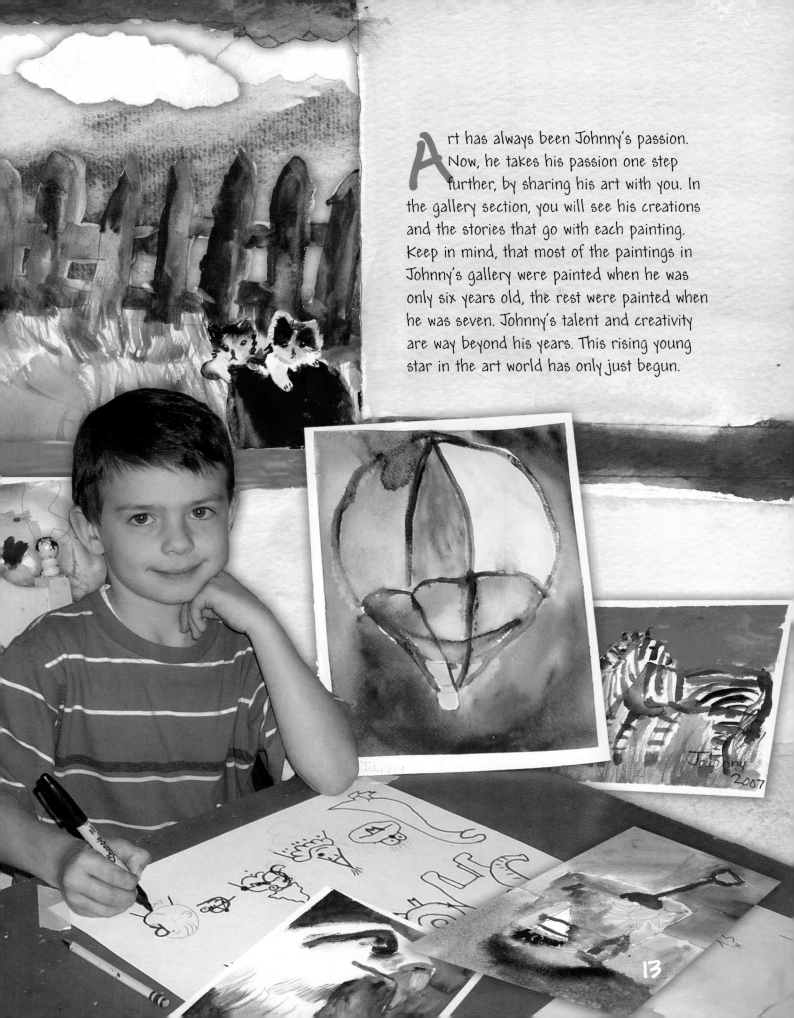

Art has always been Johnny's passion. Now, he takes his passion one step further, by sharing his art with you. In the gallery section, you will see his creations and the stories that go with each painting. Keep in mind, that most of the paintings in Johnny's gallery were painted when he was only six years old, the rest were painted when he was seven. Johnny's talent and creativity are way beyond his years. This rising young star in the art world has only just begun.

13

14

Peper & Chip

I like the part about Peper and Chip because they have a reddish / orangish mouth and their furry heads.

16

Johnny

Pete

I painted Pete thinking about Richard because he loves Parrots.

Frinsis

My favorite part about Frinsis is his dark green, blackish eyes, his pink ears and the white and gray body. This was a dog that my uncle and aunt had named Spencer.

18

Johnny

Johnny

Fruit Table

I love fruit. That is why I
painted this picture.

Lighthouse

I like lighthouses. I want to go to
one some day.

Johnny 2007

Pear Dice Beach

I have been to a beach just like this. I found
lots of shells on the beach. I really like going
to the beach. It is fun!

Jackson

He is my dog. Half his face is white,
and the other half is brown. Jackson
(Jack) is my first dog.

20

22

Sweet Dreams

I chose this picture to paint
because they were so cute.

Friends

I like the part about friends because they
are hugging each other, I like the
different ways the stripes are, and the
long grass in the picture.

Stretch

I picked out this picture in art class,
and painted Stretch, a Giraffe.

24

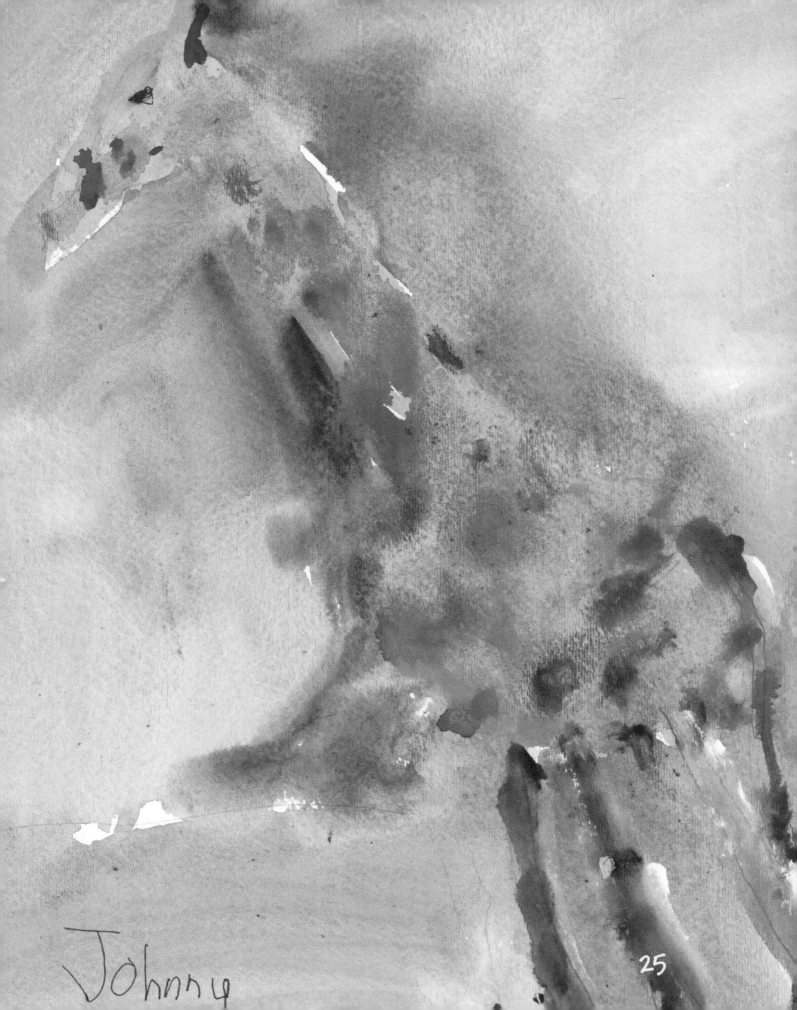

Johnny

25

Bubble Whale

What I like about the Bubble Whale, is
that he has bubbles all over him.

Beach Bucket

I painted this in my art class. My
teacher, Miss Annette put a bucket in
front of me, and I painted it.

January House

I named this January because I painted it in January and we had a lot of snow just like this.

JanJohn
2009

30

Tom

I painted this police car and gave him eyes. This way he would be alive. I named
the car Tom because my neighbor in Las Vegas was a retired police officer. His
name was Tom, and we talked about police stuff all the time!

Johnny
32

Johnny

This was painted for my new book,
"My Saturday Adventure.

Summer Fun

We are having summer fun in Grammy's
pool.... These are me and my cousins on
our inner tubes.

33

John
2001

34

I have an orange fish, in a glass bowl
that looks like a bubble.

Johnny
2007

Chimp

I like chimp because he has yellow
brownish whiskers, and I like the log
he's standing on.

Up Up and Away

I have always liked hot air balloons. On the
way to my Mom's work one day, I saw some
hot air balloons, and always wanted to go
on one. So, I painted it.

36

Johnny

38

My Papa, my Mom's Dad has horses in his field. I always liked to feed them apples, so I painted this picture. This was my 2nd painting in my art class.

Bird Neighborhood

I chose four bird houses to paint from pictures in Miss Annette's class.

39

Ginger Snow Man

I painted this for my Mom. I made this snowman in my back yard and then it melted. I wanted to save it so I painted it.

Peek-a-boo Cat

I named this cat Peek-A-Boo because he looks like he is peeking over the table.

Grilisy

My favorite part about Grilisy Bear is the trees, because they have some reddish colors to them. I like the shadows on the bear.

42

Flip Flops

I painted these flip flops with the help of my brother, Brett. I used his feet for the painting, and it was used in my book, **My Saturday Adventure**.

2008 Jan Johnny

Cat in the Mailbox

When I look at this, I think maybe it was around Christmas time. A cat was waiting in the mailbox for his letter from Santa.

Wicked Wizard

The best part of the painting is the owl that I put in there. I got the idea from seeing it in a book. The hands on the wizard are the best I've ever painted (This was my 1st painting I did in art class.)

46

Back in the 50s

This was one of the paintings I did in the first week of art class. I picked out a picture from Miss Annette's class, and painted it.

49

50

Johnn
04

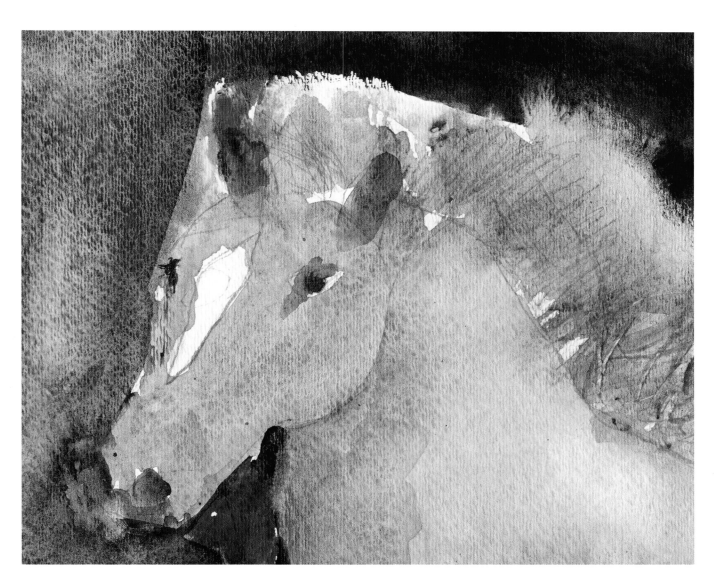

Thunder Horse

This is another horse from Papa's field. I used a credit card to make the mane on his back look real.

The Alien Spy

He is an Alien Spy and he came to earth from Mars to take pictures of us. He is spying on us.

Grammy's Whiskers

I painted this picture of a cat as a present for my Grammy. When she saw it, she told me to make the whiskers longer, so I called it Grammy's Whiskers.

54

The Climbing Guy

I made up the climber who is climbing Mount Spokane. I always wondered how far up he goes.

Freedom

I like his shiny orange beak and his greenish bluish eyes.

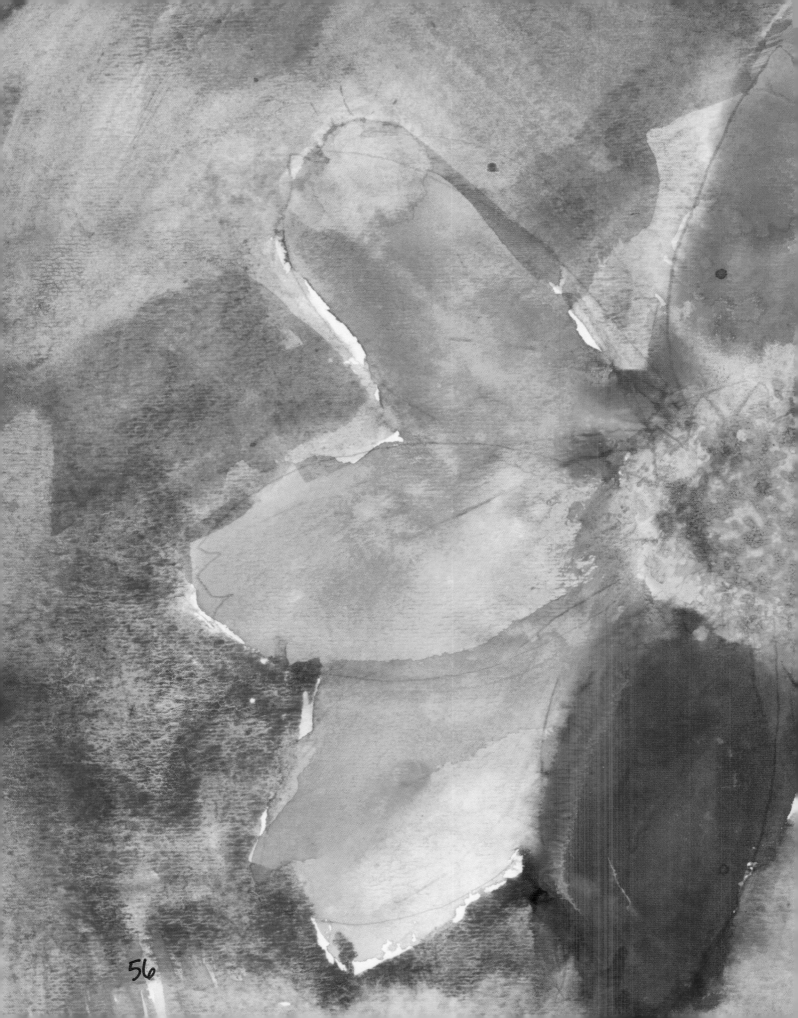

Nine Flowers

I named it Nine Flower because it has 9 petals on it. On the original, I put salt on it to make it look and feel like a real flower.

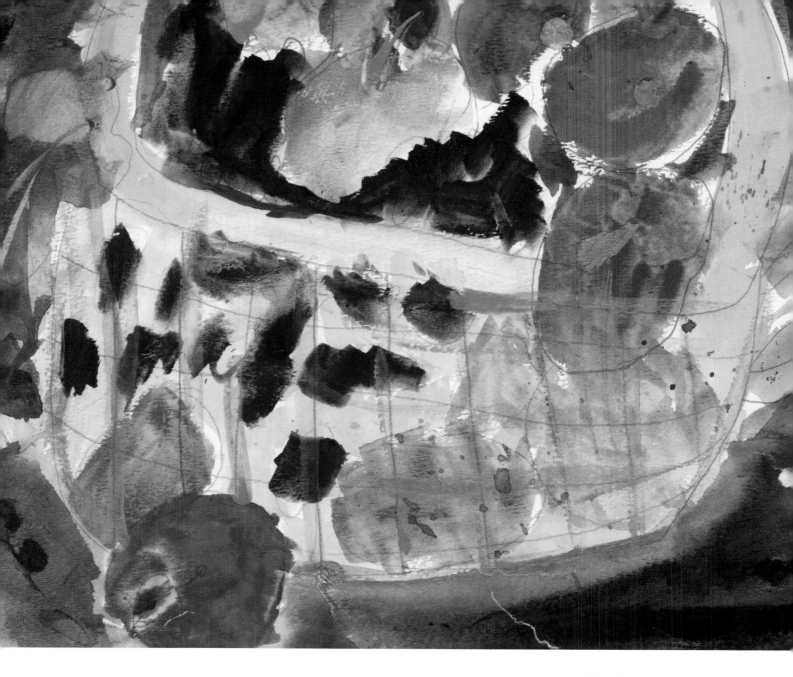

The Fruit Basket

I like fruit and grapes, apples, oranges, and bananas, so I went and painted this fruit basket.

58

The Flower Pot

This was in my backyard.

60

Johnny
2008

Cheesey

I named him Cheesey
because he is a cheese color.

One Night

I chose to draw this from a painting in
Richard's book. It is one of my favorites.

MY SATURDAY ADVENTURE

The first in the Johnny's Adventure Books Series

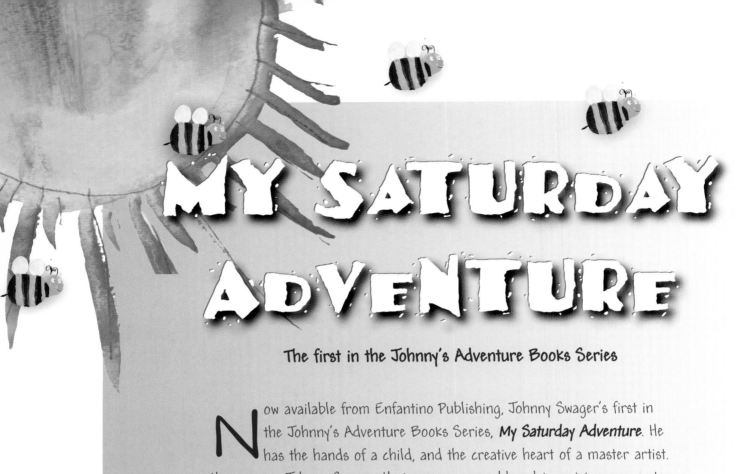

Now available from Enfantino Publishing, Johnny Swager's first in the Johnny's Adventure Books Series, **My Saturday Adventure**. He has the hands of a child, and the creative heart of a master artist. His name is Johnny Swager. He is seven years old and is a rising young star in the world of art. Born September 4, 2000, he grew up in Las Vegas, NV, and now resides with his family in Liberty Lake, WA.

Art has always been Johnny's passion. Now, he takes his passion one step further by writing and illustrating his first book, **My Saturday Adventure**, a story that reflects the purity and innocence of a child.

Johnny Swager is about to set the art world on its ear with a view of life as seen through the eyes of a seven year old.

See more of my artwork at
www.johnnyart.com

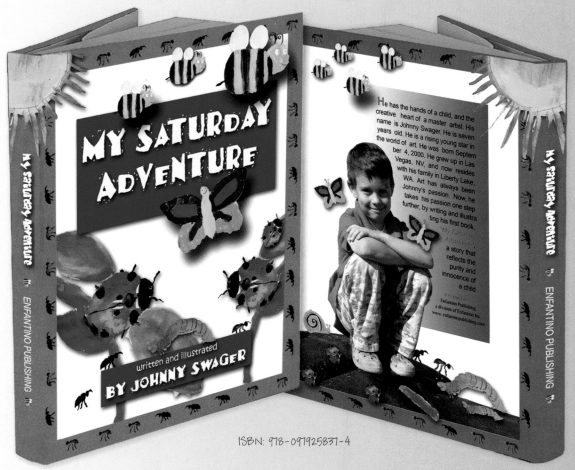

ISBN: 978-097925837-4

Available at your local book store or on line at
www.johnnyart.com or www.artbuyerimru.com

63

Index to Painings

Johnny
2001